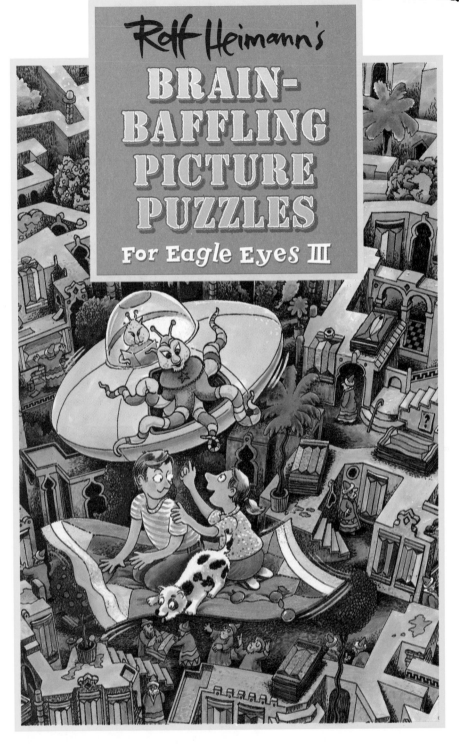

# Rolf Heimann's
# BRAIN-BAFFLING PICTURE PUZZLES
## For Eagle Eyes III

Troll

Published by arrangement with Roland Harvey Books, Port Melbourne, Victoria, Australia.

First U.S. Edition published 1999.

Printed in the United States of America.

ISBN 0-8167-5035-1

10 9 8 7 6 5 4 3 2 1

Think you have the eyes of an eagle? Test them out on the thirteen picture puzzles in this book. Read each story and then try to find the things asked for. When you think you have the answers, you can check them at the end of the book... where you'll find another bunch of questions to puzzle you.

Once upon a time there were six little dwarfs. They were called Sloppy, Creepy, Nutty, Leaky, Bloopy, and Vladimir Vissarionovitch Knopfelmacher. Along with their names, they had another problem. Every time they returned from a trip to the Tragic Mushroom Forest, they found that at least one of them had been bitten by a Blue Adder. Luckily, they had an effective treatment against the bite of the deadly snake. It was made from a certain type of mushroom, which could be recognized by the special arrangement of rings on its stem. Their problem was that each time they went into the mushroom forest to cut down a mushroom as an antidote, one of them got bitten and they had to go back to get another mushroom, only to find that one of them had been bitten again. To end this vicious cycle they decided to take home a second mushroom. But it had to have exactly the same pattern of rings as the one already on the ground.

*Is there another mushroom the same?*

As Ken and Karla rubbed the dirt from the old bottle, the stopper popped out and a thick cloud of purple smoke poured from it.

"You owe me three wishes," growled the giant genie. "If you cannot fulfill them I shall cut you into little pieces."

"I think you have it wrong," Ken said with a laugh. "You owe *us* three wishes."

"No!" thundered the genie. "You rubbed me the wrong way! Listen carefully now…"

"Your first wish is granted, master," mocked Ken. "I'm listening."

"What? Oh, that didn't count," mumbled the baffled genie.

"Oh, yes, it does," said Ken. "It always does when it's the other way around, doesn't it?"

"I wish you would not always interrupt me!" thundered the giant genie. He immediately realized he had just expressed another wish and waited for Ken to interrupt him again. But Ken was no fool. He just nodded to show that the second wish was granted!

Knowing he had only one wish left, the giant genie said, "Listen. I've been in that tiny bottle for a thousand years, and now I want another container. Find me one! I don't care what it looks like as long as it has the colors of my turban, namely red, green, blue, and orange."

Ken and Karla could not find such a container, yet they found a solution.

*Could you?*

3

Every day at noon an iron ball was lowered from Pink Tower, so that the captains of all ships in the harbor could set their clocks by it. Lowering the ball was a rather boring job, but Alexander Graham Zweistein, the keeper of the ball, had made it more interesting by inventing a machine to do it for him. When he interviewed five applicants for the position of Assistant Noonball Controller, he gave them all a test. "Watch closely," he said. "If I explode the balloon, the noise will scare Purple Nessie here so that she'll pull the rope away. But if I lure her with this fish, she'll come closer, loosening the rope. Which should I do to make the Noonball drop? The position of Assistant Noonball Controller will go to the first person who gives me the correct answer!"

*Which action will lower the Noonball?*

It was Lina's first day as a waitress in the famous Bamboo Palace restaurant in Bali, which prided itself on its excellent food and outstanding service. That's why it was important that the right dishes were always delivered to the right tables.

The orders had already been written down and marked: "American," "Japanese," "German," "Danish," and "Australian." Would Lina find the different nationalities without asking?

The owner had told Lina, "Since you're new here, I don't think you'll get them all right the first time. But I expect you to get three out of five. If not, I can't use you!"

*Would you be able to guess at least three of the different nationalities?*

**5**

"Impossible!" cried Rita. "You can't remove tattoos by hypnosis!"

"Go away, kid," said the owner of the shop, who didn't want to lose a customer.

Roger the biker wanted to have the name "LIL" removed from his tattoo. "My new girlfriend's name is Metea," he explained, "and she wants to see her own name."

"How does it work?" asked Rita.

"Go away, kid," the owner repeated. "The machine is basically an amplifier of hypowaves, using submolecular remodulation."

"Makes sense," said Roger the biker, who wasn't very bright.

"We can do it while you wait," offered the operator. "And it's almost painless. You'll merely feel a slight discomfort as my assistant applies the concussionette to your cranial area."

"Ouch!" cried Roger as the concussionette was applied. He even passed out for a minute. When he came to, he exclaimed, "But the name is still there!"

"Well, of course it is," explained the operator. "With hypnosis it will take two or three days for the letters to disappear, and for the image-resistance to take effect."

"Of course," said Roger the biker, picking up his leather jacket. "How much do I owe you?…Oh, I seem to have forgotten my wallet."

Rita couldn't contain herself any longer. "Come to the police with me," she said. "I can tell them how your wallet disappeared!"

*Could you tell how it vanished?*

Professor Smyth was on a field trip when he found the road blocked by a flooded creek. Soon another car arrived. Its driver introduced himself as Possum.

Sitting by the evening fire, the professor suggested, "Why don't we play a game? We'll ask each other questions, and whoever can't answer pays the other a dollar."

"Good idea," agreed Possum. "Except, being a city slicker and having gone to school and all, you probably know much more than I do. So it wouldn't be fair. What if I pay only twenty cents for your dollar?"

The professor felt flattered.

"Okay," he said with a laugh. "You go first."

Possum asked, "What has three legs and one eye?"

The professor didn't know and paid a dollar.

"What has four legs but can't stand up?" asked Possum.

Again the professor didn't know and paid a dollar.

"What has only one leg and a spotted head?"

"Don't know," admitted the professor, paying his dollar. "But now let me take a turn. First tell me, what are all these things with different legs?"

"Don't know either," said Possum. "Here's my twenty cents."

*Everything Possum described is in fact nearby. Could you have found them and saved the professor's money?*

**7**

Xip the clown and Arturo the human cannonball did not like each other.

"You're nothing but a clown," Arturo often said.

"And you're nothing but a dumb human cannonball," Xip replied.

Things came to a head one day when Xip couldn't find his pants. "You stole them!" he accused Arturo. "You want people to laugh at me, don't you?"

"In case you've forgotten," Arturo answered, "you're a clown. People are supposed to laugh at you." Suddenly he grew serious. "Where are my lucky red goggles?" he demanded. "You took them!"

"What a daredevil!" mocked Xip. "Needs his lucky red goggles, huh? Needs his mommy, too, I'll bet?"

"That's it!" exclaimed Arturo. "I challenge you to a duel!"

"Choose your weapons!" Xip cried.

"Cannons!" bellowed Arturo. This wasn't possible, since the circus had only one cannon. So Xip chose to ride Oscar the legless snake instead. Xip was the only one who could handle the vicious reptile.

The duel was staged as a big show.

"Adults can be so childish," said Frank to his sister Lucy. "Some-body is going to get hurt unless we find Xip's pants and Arturo's lucky red goggles."

*Can you find Xip's pants and Arturo's red goggles?*

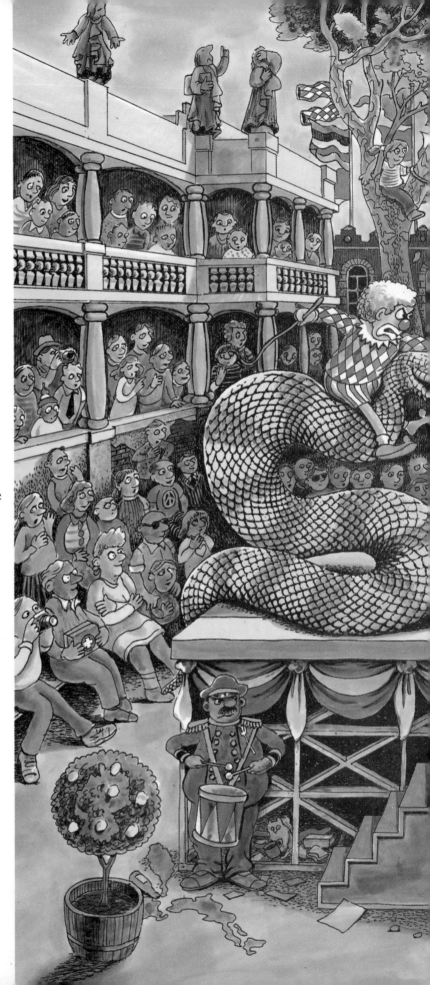

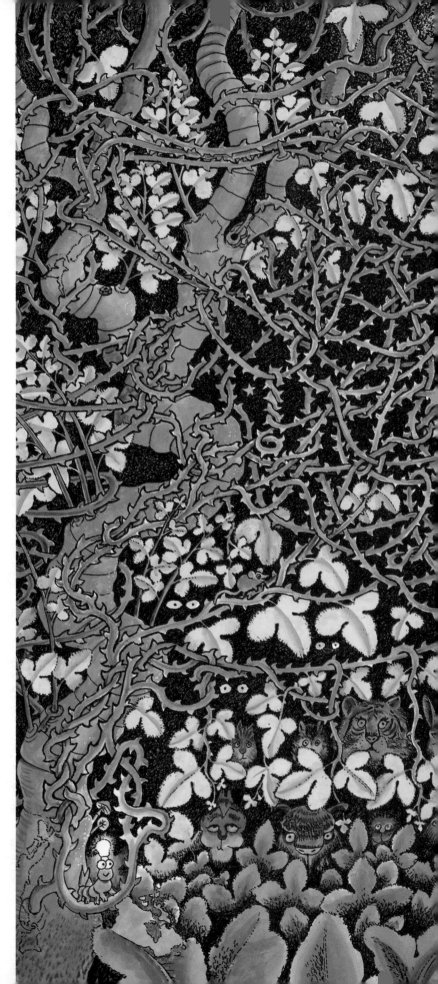

The jungle of South Transmonia was a strange place. Take the Swallowtailed glow worm (Tailus Swallonia Heimanii), for instance. The red female could only move along the red branches of the Transmonian thorn vine, whereas the green male could only move along green vines. One step on a vine of the wrong color and they would suffer severe foot itch. It was their practice to meet at full moon for a songfest. The problem was that they had to meet each other on neutral ground, namely a yellow leaf. Of course, it had to be a yellow leaf that could be reached by both a red vine and a green vine.

*Is there such a leaf?*

Mita was the first to see the two aliens in their bright green flying saucer. "Hey there!" she called. "I bet you want us to take you to our leader?"

"Not at all," said the alien. "We've had bad experiences with leaders. That's why we prefer the common people. Are your common?"

"Are we?" wondered Mita. "I guess we are…"

Her brother Matt disagreed. "I don't think you can call us common, since we're flying on a magic carpet!"

"That's what I want to ask you about," said the alien. "What kind of fuel do you use for this craft, and is it expensive?"

"This type of vehicle runs on pure imagination," explained Mita. "If you don't have imagination, forget it and stick to your conventional saucers."

"Imagination we have," said the alien. "But where can we buy one of these things?"

"You're in luck," said Mita. "Below is the famous magic carpet market of Mahred-El-Rashun. But don't buy just any carpet. Buy one that has the same design and colors as ours. I think there's one left!"

*Can you see the carpet Mita is talking about?*

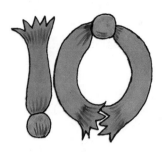

Having arrived on the planet of Turox, the astronauts found some strange life forms: a chickenoid, a humanoid, and a tapewormenoid. They turned on their translatomatic and said, "We come in peace. We have heard about the amazing purple twinberries that grow here. Our mission is to check them out and to take some back. Are they safe to eat?"

"Ah, those twinberries," said the chickenoid. "Most of them just give you hallucinations."

"We don't need that," said one astronaut. "I already feel like I'm seeing things. How can we tell which berries are good?"

"Not those that grow between green sections," said the humanoid. "First they make your skin turn a hideous white color, and before they kill you, they make hair grow from the top of your head."

"Oh, how terrible," said the other astronaut. They had been trained to be as polite as possible when confronting alien life forms. "But can you tell us which of the berries *are* edible? We can't go back empty-handed!"

"Only those that grow between red sections of the twinberry plant," said the humanoid. "But you'll be lucky to find one, because they're the ones we usually eat. Although we have been known to eat the wrong ones."

*Would you be able to find the right berries?*

It was the first time Tina had tried out her new time machine, and she got quite a surprise when she slowed down for a soft landing!
"I can't believe it!" she cried. "Is this caveman riding a dinosaur? There's something wrong here. Dinosaurs were supposedly extinct when people appeared on Earth." She called out to the caveman, "What's your name?"

"My name is Gloork," answered the boy. "I'll say there's something wrong here. Your time machine seems to be a dud."

"Why, I assembled it myself from a kit," said Tina. "What can possibly be wrong?"

"Plenty," said Gloork. "You must have your wires mixed, and because of that your time zones are all jumbled up. For instance, aren't you surprised that I speak modern English?"

"Not at all," said Tina. "Cavemen always do in the movies."

Gloork laughed. "And the saddle I'm sitting on," he pointed out. "Saddles weren't invented until much later. If you look around, you'll see a dozen things that prove your times have been mixed up!"

*Can you see them, too?*

Kate had just bought herself a pair of fashionable leg warmers. They were so comfortable and warm that she was never seen without them, even when she went to the community swimming pool. Imagine her disappointment when she came back to the locker room and found that somebody had mixed up another pair of leg warmers with hers. Now she was stuck with a mismatched pair. Hers were original Petagold Voolies, the best on the market, and they had been custom-made for her in white and green, which were the colors of her Twainball team.

It was no wonder she kept looking at everybody else's leg warmers, in the hope of finding the person responsible. She was sure it was only a matter of time until she located the missing leg warmer.

*Can you see who has mixed up the leg warmers?*

Emperor Krraakk from the planet of Kkrrookk was organizing an intergalactic food festival. His agents had already collected twinberries from the planet of Turox, sour-schnops from Boranus III, and fried tasselworms from El Sympuus. But, as everybody knows, one should never eat Sympuusian tasselworms without some sour gherkins from the planet Earth. "Go to Earth and find a place called the Spreewald," Krraakk told his Royal Food Collector. "But don't bring just any old gherkins. If I remember correctly, the best ones come from a little farm that has a yellow-flowering bush nearby and a storks' nest on the roof. If I'm not mistaken, there's also a doghouse and one or two pine trees. That's all I remember. Don't bring gherkins from anywhere else or I'll have your tentacles cut off and served as pickled calamari fritters." Even though he knew his tentacles would grow again, the Royal Food Collector was eager to avoid the indignity of having his tentacles served on the emperor's table, so he took special care to look for the right place!

*Can you find it?*

They found such a mushroom (directly behind Creepy with his clipboard). Alas, just as they expected, one of the dwarfs would be bitten again! The dwarfs would be well advised to check each item of their clothing before going home!

Unable to see any container in the required colors, the children found the following solution: they took the large orange box directly in front of them. It already had the colors green and blue on it. If they could add some red, they would have their answer! And they remembered seeing a can of red paint. All they had to do now was to find it again – plus a brush!

By the loud explosion of the balloon, Purple Nessie was frightened off and thereby lowered the ball. But she had barely gone ten feet when the red lever on top had moved as far as it could and the whole tower came crashing down! All six people scrambled for a life ring. Were there enough for all of them?

The Japanese sitting at table 3 were easy to identify because of their Asian faces. The man at table 1 was buying a *Zeitung,* which is German for newspaper. The little girl at table 2 was reading *Orne Ojne,* and the Os had lines through them. That had to be Danish.

Lina made her first mistake at table 4. Despite the fact that the girl wore braces and the boy was reading about baseball and had the logo of the Cleveland Indians on his T-shirt, the family was not American. "You've been looking for stereotypes," the man said with a laugh. "I'm the mayor of Wagga-Wagga, and you can't get more Australian than that!"

"Oh," said Lina, "and I would have bet the people at table 5 were Australian!" The mayor of Wagga-Wagga laughed again. "You were stereotyping them as well. I happen to know that they just came back from a vacation down under, which explains their T-shirts. By the way, I've been telling my kids that the noise we hear is a gecko, but we can't see it."

"We usually have three geckos here," said Lina, "and if you look closely enough, you'll find them."

Rita had seen a little green hand coming from behind the curtain and silently removing the wallet from the jacket. "And as far as the tattoo is concerned," she said, "why do you want to remove anything before writing the name of your new girlfriend? Just add a couple of letters plus a few lines to the existing ones, and presto – 'LIL' becomes 'METEA.' It's possible, you know."

The toadstool near the old car had spots on its head and only one leg, while the camera had one eye and three legs. And the crocodile had four legs but couldn't stand upright. Luckily, the two men discovered the crocodile before they were attacked!

"This place gives me the creeps," said the professor. "I always have the feeling of being watched."

"Well, we are," said Possum. "Australia's animals are mainly nocturnal."

"I don't mean the animals," said the professor. "I have the feeling the very trees themselves are watching us."

He was right. Six of them were watching!

They spotted Xip's pants on the flagpole right behind him, and the red goggles on one of the statues.

"Too late," decided Lucy. "If we stop the duel now, the crowd will go crazy, not to mention the sponsors. The best we can do is to make sure there's a first-aid kit nearby."

They found such a leaf to the left of the lion's head, only to discover that they had forgotten the little ukulele they always used to accompany themselves. One of them had to go find it and bring it back.

After looking around, the aliens spotted the same carpet under the yellow-flowering tree. They decided to land their craft on the helipad marked with a big H. But would they find their way from there to the carpet they wanted to buy?

They found an edible twinberry between red sections right on the very top of the plant.

"Just for comparison," suggested the humanoid, "you should also take a deadly one. As I said, they grow between green sections of the plant. They're hard to find but, if you're a true scientist, don't give up!"

"Well, I recognize the crablike animals below me. They're trilobites," said Tina. "Prehistoric animals happen to be my hobby. Trilobites were common in the Cambrian age, some 600 million years ago."

"If your hobby is the ancient world," said Gloork, "you might also recognize that owl-like figure underneath you as coming from the Chang Dynasty. It's about 600 years old."

As they looked around, they found quite a few other things that did not fit into the same time period. They saw the *Spirit of St. Louis,* the plane that Charles Lindbergh used to cross the Atlantic Ocean in 1927, and it was giving some Roman soldiers the surprise of their lives! A tank from modern times was being inspected by a group of soldiers who could be identified as crusaders from the Middle Ages. One was being photographed, and photography was not invented until the nineteenth century. There was also litter from the twentieth century: a can, a bottle, and so on.

"You'd better check your time machine carefully," said Gloork. "For example, are you sure the red contacts are properly connected to the blue ones? That's a common mistake with time machines, you know."

Kate discovered her leg warmer on a painting.

"Are you sure you have the colors right?" she asked the artist.

"I certainly am. This is an art class from the school of post-abstractive neocorrect realism. Our goal is to get everything right. I definitely remember that girl getting on a blue bus."

"A blue bus? Tell me, where does the blue bus go? What number was it?" If Kate could find out, she would be one step closer to tracing her leg warmer. As a user of public transportation, she knew that each bus line had a distinctive color.

"All I know is that it was blue," said the artist. "I couldn't say what number it was. Find out yourself!"

The Royal Food Collector took a tour through the entire Spreewald, but he could have saved himself the trouble. When he came back after two or three hours, he found that the very place he had landed fit the description perfectly! Unfortunately, the people there did not understand him when he said, "Ssllaannaa bbong kkrr nnuu plameponderkus…"

"Go and see Professor Michael John Klinkerman," they told him. "He speaks every language. He's easy to find because he's never far from his dog, a white and brown one with a black tail."